Gravity!
Do You Feel It?

by Buffy Silverman

Science Content Editor:
Kristi Lew

rourkeeducationalmedia.com

Scan for Related Titles
and Teacher Resources

Science content editor: Kristi Lew
A former high school teacher with a background in biochemistry and more than 10 years of experience in cytogenetic laboratories, Kristi Lew specializes in taking complex scientific information and making it fun and interesting for scientists and non-scientists alike. She is the author of more than 20 science books for children and teachers.

www.rourkeeducationalmedia.com

Photo credits:
Cover © mountainpix, Cover logo frog © Eric Pohl, test tube © Sergey Lazarev; Table Of Contents & Page 4© Phase-4Photography; Page 5 © Kadroff; Page 7 © greenland; Page 9 © Racheal Grazias; Page 10 © Steve Collender; Page 11 © Richard Susanto; Page 13 © Monkey Business Images; Page 14 © TRINACRIA PHOTO, jackhollingsworthcom, LLC; Page 16 © Matamu; Page 15 © Peter Hansen; Page 17 © Orla; Page 19 © paul prescott; Page 21 © oorka

Editor: Kelli Hicks

Cover and page design by Nicola Stratford, bdpublishing.com

Library of Congress Cataloging-in-Publication Data

Silverman, Buffy.
 Gravity! do you feel it? / Buffy Silverman.
    p. cm. -- (My science library)
 Includes bibliographical references and index.
 ISBN 978-1-61741-754-2 (hard cover -English)(alk. paper)
 ISBN 978-1-61741-956-0 (soft cover - English)
 ISBN 978-1-61236-677-7 (e-Book - English)
 ISBN 978-1-61236-929-7 (soft cover - Spanish)
 ISBN 978-1-62169-081-8 (e-Book - Spanish)
 1. Gravity--Juvenile literature. I. Title. II. Series.

 QC178.S467 2012
 531'.14--dc22

                          2011004841

Also Available as:

Rourke Educational Media
Printed in the United States of America,
North Mankato, Minnesota

rourkeeducationalmedia.com

customerservice@rourkeeducationalmedia.com • PO Box 643328 Vero Beach, Florida 32964

Table of Contents

What Is Gravity?

Toss a ball into the sky. No matter how hard you throw it, the ball comes back to the ground. What makes the ball return to Earth? **Gravity**!

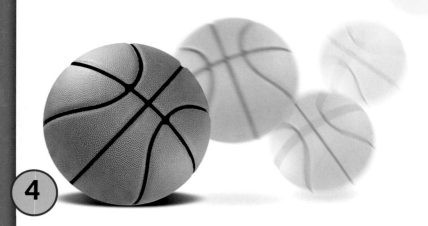

You cannot see gravity. But, you can see that it pulls a ball back to Earth.

Gravity is a **force**. A force is something that pushes or pulls an object. The Earth's gravity pulls objects towards the center of the Earth.

What would happen if there was no gravity? Rocks, houses, plants, and animals would float into space. People would float, too.

You have to work hard to climb up a climbing wall because gravity is pulling.

The force of gravity pulls all objects towards each other. Every object in the **universe** pulls on every other object.

The Earth, Sun, Moon, and **planets** pull on each other. Buildings, cars, and trains pull on each other. You have **gravitational pull**, too!

A rollercoaster zooms down a track. Gravity pulls on it as it goes up and down.

9

How Does Gravity Work?

Everything in the universe is made of **matter**. People, air, water, rocks, and planets are made of matter. Scientists call the amount of matter in an object its **mass**.

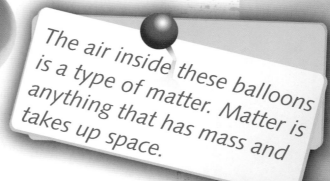

The air inside these balloons is a type of matter. Matter is anything that has mass and takes up space.

A tree has more mass than you!

Objects with more mass have more gravitational pull. The Earth has much more mass than you do. That means that the Earth pulls with more force.

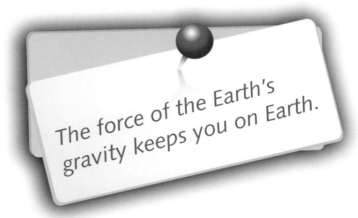

The force of the Earth's gravity keeps you on Earth.

Your **weight** is a measure of the pull of gravity between you and the Earth. The Moon is smaller than Earth and has less mass. That means that its gravity has less pull. A 70-pound (32 kilograms) child weighs only 12 pounds (5 kilograms) on the Moon.

"On Earth I weigh 70 pounds or 32 kilograms."

"On the Moon I weigh 12 pounds or 5 kilograms."

When astronauts went to the Moon, they weighed less than on Earth.

Orbiting in Space

Objects in space pull each other together. The Sun has much more mass than the Earth. Its gravity is stronger. The Sun has a greater pull than Earth. It holds the Earth in place as the Earth moves in an **orbit** around the Sun.

The Sun makes up 99.86% of the mass of the solar system. It pulls on all the planets. The planets orbit the Sun.

The Sun's gravity holds the planets in the solar system.

Earth

Sun

The Earth has more mass than the Moon. Its gravity is stronger. The Earth's gravity pulls more than the Moon's gravity. The Moon orbits the Earth. It cannot escape Earth's gravity.

Gravity pulls the Earth and Moon together.

The force of gravity also depends on the distance between two objects. Planets that are far apart have less pull on each other. Imagine traveling far from any moons, planets, or stars. There would be almost no gravity pulling on you. Then you could float away!

Mars

Moon

Earth

Mars is farther from Earth than the Moon. There is less gravitational pull between Mars and Earth.

21

Show What You Know

1. What would happen if the Earth had no gravity?

2. Why is there less gravity on the Moon than on Earth?

3. How would your weight change if you visited a planet with more mass than Earth?

Glossary

force (FORS): something that pulls or pushes something else

gravitational pull (GRAV-uh-TA-shun-ul PULL): the force that pulls objects together

gravity (GRAV-uh-tee): a force that pulls matter together

mass (MASS): the amount of matter that an object contains

matter (MAT-ur): anything that has mass and takes up space

orbit (OR-bit): the path of an object as it revolves around a planet or sun

planets (PLAN-its): large bodies, such as Earth, that revolve around a star

universe (YOO-nih-vurss): the Earth, planets, stars, and all things that exist in space

weight (WATE): a measure of the pull of gravity between an object and Earth or another planet

Index

Websites

www.exploratorium.edu/ronh/weight/index.html

www.historyforkids.org/scienceforkids/physics/space/gravity.htm

www.primarygames.com/arcade/gravity/start.htm

www.sciencenetlinks.com/interactives/gravity.html

About the Author

Buffy Silverman tries to beat gravity when she hikes and bicycles. When she's not exploring the great outdoors, she writes about science and nature.

Meet The Author!
www.meetREMauthors.com